SCHOLASTIC

REAL-LIFE MATHS

Ten ways to teach key maths concepts in rich and relevant scenarios

AGES to 11

Aubergines
50p each
5 for £2

Red Peppers
30p each
4 for £1

Chillies
30p Each
10 for £2

Tomatoes
40p each
or 3 for £1

Shopping List

Tomatoes £1·80
Chillies £2·00
Red Peppers £1·00
Aubergines £3·00

Total £7·80

Includes FREE CD-ROM

SCHOLASTIC

Book End, Range Road, Witney, Oxfordshire, OX29 OYD
www.scholastic.co.uk
© 2013, Scholastic Ltd
1 2 3 4 5 6 7 8 9   0 1 2 3 4 5 6 7 8 9

British Library Cataloguing-in-Publication Data
A catalogue record for this book is available from the
British Library.

ISBN 978-1407-12793-4
Printed by Bell & Bain Ltd, Glasgow

Text © Paul Hollin 2013

Commissioning Editor
Paul Naish

Development Editor
Emily Jefferson

Editor
Mary Nathan

Proofreader
Kate Pedlar

Series Designer
Shelley Best

Illustrator
Paul Hutchinson

Acknowledgements
The publishers gratefully acknowledge permission
to reproduce the following copyright material:

Cover: vegetables © Ragip Candan/iStockphoto.com
Page 13: window 1 © Paul Erickson/Photo's.com,
window 2 © Hemera Technologies/Photo's.com,
window 3 © Dynamic Graphics/Photo's.com
Page 25: gym © Leremy/Shutterstock.com
Page 38: world of numbers © Nikolaas Boden/
iStockphoto.com

About the author
Paul Hollin worked for many years in teaching,
starting as a maths tutor for the Home Tutors
Teachers' Cooperative in London. After stints doing
photography in youth clubs and teaching English in
Spain and London, he eventually became a primary
teacher working mainly with junior-aged children.
He left the classroom to work for Sherston
Software, where he designed a wide range
of educational software and now works in
educational publishing, writing and providing
consultancy in a freelance capacity.

Contents

REAL-LIFE MATHS Ages 9–11

About the series

Real-Life Maths is a series of three books designed to supplement your maths curriculum. Each book provides a wide range of extended scenarios that develop many maths skills in engaging and meaningful contexts, often involving significant child interaction. The three books are categorised by age range, although teachers will find materials suitable for their classes across the series as the activities are relatively age neutral. The planning grids for the books are available on each respective CD-ROM.

The importance of real-life maths

Anyone who keeps their eye on the educational news will know that maths is a hot topic: standards aren't good enough; adults can't add up; other countries do it better, and so on. Why is it thus? It is interesting to compare maths with literacy; between the two they form the bedrock of primary education. There are many technical aspects to developing a child's capabilities in literacy – these are sometimes taught discretely and sometimes integrated. Either way, every primary school in the land uses real sources of language, such as books, newspapers and drama, to aid pupils' literacy development; not to mention the myriad of approaches for writing in context – letters, stories, poems, and more.

Now look at maths. The majority of maths lessons involve the discrete teaching of specific skills, be it the four operations, factors, or shape. The nature of maths dictates this to some extent, but it can leave those being taught it fundamentally baffled – why are they learning it? Now, *we* know why – being numerate is essential in adult life – but, and here's the crux of the matter, in adult life nearly all of us use our numeracy skills in meaningful situations. These books do not suggest that you should fundamentally alter your maths curriculum, but by simply adding a regular dose of real-life maths, as well as engaging and motivating your pupils, they will see the point of it all. Real-life maths activities are not just about getting the right answers. Mistakes can be useful, allowing children to see that the consequence of an error is not simply a cross and a correction: an error might result in an incorrect design, getting lost, or even losing money.

About the activities

There are ten real-life scenarios per book, each one providing a multi-session, structured scenario complete with teacher guidance and resources on paper and the accompanying CD-ROM. Typically, a scenario will take between two and four lessons to complete. Every scenario has a practical focus, where the maths is an integral part of a greater task – just like life!

The scenarios are arranged in roughly increasing levels of difficulty, and between them they cover a wide range of maths skills, often with several skills being involved in any one activity. In addition, because of their focus on the real world, the scenarios have cross-curricular links, and most primary subjects are covered.

The activities are all fairly challenging. They require extended thinking and clear organisation of work, as well as making demands on children's mathematical thinking. Some can be done by individuals, though many would benefit from paired or group work, and some involve whole-class participation in highly 'immersive' situations.

Scenario content

Each scenario covers four pages in the book, and typically consists of:

1. Teacher notes

Mathematics coverage; guidance on organising and running lessons; tips for differentiation; review and further ideas.

2. Scenario guidelines

Introducing the scenario; guidelines and 'rules'; additional information; worked examples where appropriate.

3. Resources and information

Typically this page has all of the mathematical and factual information needed to run the scenario.

4. Recording sheet

Typically this page provides a template for children to use to lay out their work, though sometimes additional paper is required.

CD-ROM content

For every activity there is extensive supporting material on the CD-ROM, including an introductory video and slideshow, which set the scene. In addition, all photocopiables are available on the CD-ROM for easy printing. Most activities have further support sheets which can be printed, and some have additional resources, such as simple chart and graphing tools.

Planning and running real-life maths sessions

Good learning and good lessons come at a price – real-life maths scenarios require preparation. Teachers will need to familiarise themselves with the scenario in advance, as well as prepare resources.

How you weave the lessons into your curriculum will depend on your general approach to teaching. Do you want to challenge children by presenting activities that are in their 'zone of development', or do you prefer to consolidate well-honed skills?

Typically, the first lesson is about introducing the scenario to the class. There is an introduction for each activity on the CD-ROM which, while not essential, does provide a clear overview of the context and situation. In addition, introducing or recapping the key maths skills involved is encouraged. Children may also need to do some planning in advance of the second lesson.

The second lesson is where the scenario really gets underway. Ideally, having more than an hour available would be useful if things are progressing well. However long you spend, a plenary review is encouraged afterwards, where broader issues of the purpose of the maths as well as the maths skills involved can be discussed.

Subsequent lessons, either repetitions with variation or extensions, are also possible at your discretion – and if you are inspired there are ideas for further work in the teacher notes for each scenario, as well as guidance at the back of the book.

Remember, the activities in all three books are relatively age neutral in tone, and can be used effectively to challenge or support children in other age groups, and all three books' planning grids are on the CD-ROM.

Ages 9–11	Pages 8–11	Pages 12–15	Pages 16–19	Pages 20–23	Pages 24–27
Scenario	1. MonarchQuest	2. Stained-glass designers	3. Decathletes	4. Market day	5. In the gym
Focus	A game to arrange the kings and queens of England in order and calculate era lengths.	Designing and costing bespoke stained-glass windows according to specific requirements.	Pupils take part in a virtual decathlon, with random results generation every time.	Pupils take on the roles of wholesalers, stallholders or customers at Middletown market.	Pupils create exercise programs and monitor progress for a range of gym members.
Difficulty rating (3 max.)	★	★★	★★	★	★★
Maths covered	● Ordering numbers between 1000 and 2000 ● Finding differences between larger numbers	● Understanding shape ● Measuring and calculating areas ● Symmetry and scale ● Calculating costs	● Using formulae ● Multiplying up to 1000 ● Adding up to 10,000 ● Checking work with a calculator	● Using appropriate operations ● Money	● Reading charts ● Estimating ● Adding/subtracting HTU ● Presentation of work
Cross-curricular links	● Literacy: speaking and listening ● History: chronology of English monarchs	● Literacy: speaking and listening ● Art: creating designs	● ICT: data handling ● PE: sport awareness	● Literacy: speaking and listening ● PSHE: healthy eating; financial awareness	● Science, PE and PSHE: healthy living and the functioning of the heart and body
CD-ROM material	● Introductory slideshow ● PDFs of photocopiables ● Alternative date strips ● Complete monarch dates	● Introductory slideshow ● PDFs of photocopiables ● Grid paper	● Introductory slideshow ● Random results generator ● PDFs of photocopiables ● Decathlon point system	● Introductory slideshow ● PDFs of photocopiables ● Illustrations of all goods ● Illustrations of money ● Transaction tracking sheet	● Introductory slideshow ● PDFs of photocopiables ● Large versions of charts ● Useful links
Resources needed	Photocopiables, pencils and paper	Photocopiables, pencils, squared paper, rulers, compasses, coloured pencils/pens	Photocopiables, pencils, paper, calculators	Photocopiables, pencils, felt pens, paper	Photocopiables, pencils and paper
Timescales	Minimum two lessons, at least one hour each	Minimum two lessons, at least one hour each	Minimum two lessons, at least one hour each	Minimum two lessons, at least one hour each	Minimum two lessons, at least one hour each
Organisation	Teams of one to four; lots of movement	Individual, paired or small groups	Individual, paired or small groups	Whole-class, pupils in 'role'; lots of movement	Individual, paired or small groups

Ages 9–11 continued	Pages 28–31	Pages 32–35	Pages 36–39	Pages 40–43	Pages 44–47
Scenario	6. Beautiful bathrooms	7. Global city-dash 3000	8. A world of statistics	9. Four-a-side football	10. Dragonmasters
Focus	Pupils must design and cost a range of bathrooms to fit different customers' needs.	A race around the globe visiting each continent once, stopping at capital cities.	Pupils must present complex information in easy-to-understand formats to compare countries.	Pupils participate in a mini-league, using probability to decide events.	Groups work together to build shelters strong enough to resist dragon attacks.
Difficulty rating (3 max.)	★★	★★★	★★★	★	★★★
Maths covered	• Four operations • Adding money to £1000+ • Calculating areas • Clear and logical presentation of work	• Calculating distances using larger numbers • Time (24 hours) • Approximating • Reading charts	• Using and rounding larger numbers • Percentages and fractions • Data handling and interpretation	• Adding numbers with one decimal place up to 10 • Basic probability	• Using formulae • Using four operations up to and over 1000 • Working methodically • Strategic thinking
Cross-curricular links	• Literacy: speaking and listening • D&T: design • PSHE: financial awareness	• Literacy: speaking and listening • Geography: awareness of world geography	• Literacy: speaking and listening • Geography: global understanding • ICT: data handling	• Literacy: speaking and listening • ICT: data handling • PE: sport awareness	• Literacy: speaking and listening • PSHE: cooperation
CD-ROM material	• Introductory slideshow • PDFs of photocopiables • Sample costing, design and estimate	• Introductory slideshow • PDFs of photocopiables • World maps	• Introductory slideshow • PDFs of photocopiables • Data handling tools • Useful links	• Introductory slideshow • PDFs of photocopiables • Player data • Pitch and league templates • Sample gameplay	• Introductory slideshow • PDFs of photocopiables
Resources needed	Photocopiables, pencils, paper, rulers and calculators (optional)	Photocopiables, maps and globes (optional), pencils, paper, rulers, calculators (optional)	Photocopiables, pencils and paper, atlases and globes, internet access (optional)	Photocopiables, pencils, dice, coins, counters, team charts, pitch plans, whistle (optional)	Photocopiables, pencils, paper, calculators (optional)
Timescales	Minimum three lessons, around one hour each	Minimum two lessons, at least one hour each	Minimum three lessons, one hour per lesson	Minimum three lessons, around one hour each	Minimum three lessons, at least one hour each
Organisation	Individual, paired or small groups	Pairs or small groups	Individual, paired or small groups	Groups of four, rotating regularly	Groups of around four pupils

MonarchQuest

Overview
Children arrange the kings and queens of England in order and calculate reigns and eras as fast as possible. This activity provides practice in ordering numbers between 1000 and 2000, and in calculating differences between larger numbers.

Timescales
- Lesson 1 (maximum 1 hour): Introduce activity and rules, and develop familiarity with how monarchs' reigns and eras are described.
- Lesson 2 (about 1 hour): Play the game in full.
- Repeating the game: A second playing of the game will be easier, but add tension by reducing the time available and ensuring children receive different date lists.
- Extension: Ask children to research exact dates, and calculate the lengths of reigns in days.

Maths covered
- Ordering numbers between 1000 and 2000.
- Finding differences between larger numbers.

Prior learning
Children should be familiar with ordering, adding and finding differences between larger numbers.

Cross-curricular links
- Literacy: speaking and listening.
- History: chronology of English monarchs.

CD-ROM resources list
- Scenario video and slideshow.
- Photocopiables: Scenario guidelines, Monarch date strips, Dates recording sheet, Alternative date strips, Lists of royal houses.

Resource list
Pencils, paper.

Setting the scene
Explain that children will be playing a game to organise the kings and queens of England since 1066 into their correct chronological order. During Lesson 1, provide an overview of how the history of monarchs is structured, and clarify how dates are organised. Using fictitious monarchs, model how children can use the dates that successive monarchs arrive on the throne to calculate the length of each monarch's reign. Run through methods for finding differences between larger numbers, if necessary. Watch the introduction to the game on the CD-ROM. Then follow the on-screen information to organise the monarchs.

Running the scenario
Arrange the class into teams and give each team the photocopiables Monarch date strips and Dates recording sheet. (If possible, enlarge these to A3.) Ideally, each team should have one to four children, so some teams will have the same date strips. (Note: an Alternative date strips photocopiable is also provided on the CD-ROM.) This is not a problem; although they won't be able to trade information with each other, but will have to talk to other teams instead. Discuss how each team might assign different roles. Ensure that children have organised their teams and understand the task and the rules, especially with regards to trading information. Decide on a time limit, play the introduction on the CD-ROM and start the game.

Differentiation
Less confident learners can be encouraged to use written methods for their calculations.
More confident learners should do all calculations mentally.

Review
Discuss the game itself. What was fair/unfair? What was easy/hard? What was fun/frustrating? Did children spot any tricks that help to speed up their work? If they were to play again, how would they adapt their tactics? Was trading information easy? Would they change any rules?

Further ideas
Children could make their own version of MonarchQuest for the Saxon and Viking kings (dates on photocopiable Lists of royal houses on the CD-ROM). This concept can easily be extended to other countries or time periods, for example, Ancient Egyptian pharaohs or Roman emperors.

Welcome to MonarchQuest, where fast thinking and teamwork can help you win. Will you be the first to find out how long every queen and king of England reigned for?

Aim of the game

- Each player or team starts with a jumbled list of monarchs, containing only the dates they came to the throne. Your goal is to be the first to complete all dates for all monarchs, and to calculate how long each one was on the throne.

- Each player or team has ten different monarchs missing from their list. You must talk to other players or teams to trade information – it's the only way you can complete your *Dates recording sheet*. When you are finished shout, "MonarchQuest!" If you are not first to finish, keep going until the teacher calls, "Time!" Everyone will have their work checked at the end, and errors carry penalties.

Rules

- ■ You must do the following:
- Put every monarch in the correct chronological order.
- State the dates they arrived on and left the throne. (You can only do this once you are certain who came after them.)
- Calculate how many years they were on the throne. For example: King Richard I, 1189–1199, 10 years.
- You must do the same for each house (for example, Normans).
- If you suspect that you have a monarch missing, approach another player/team and offer to trade information. **You must not look at other people's work or information lists. You can only trade information verbally, by asking questions, though you can write down responses.** For example, you might ask, "Who do you have that came after Richard III?" In response you might be asked, "Who was the first Plantagenet monarch? And when did they reign?"
- Before you start, discuss your tactics and try to organise your team effectively. Will you each deal with a certain era? Will some of you be information traders, and others calculators? Who will write down all the answers?

Points

- First player/team to finish completely scores 100 points.
- Second player/team to finish completely scores 90 points.
- Third player/team to finish completely scores 80 points.
- And so on for all teams that complete the task in time.
- Teams can score additional points for each of the following (circle the answers on your date recording sheet):
  - Identifying the longest-serving monarch scores 25 points.
  - Identifying the longest-reigning house scores 25 points.
  - Identifying when there were two monarchs ruling at the same time scores 25 points.
  - Identifying the three monarchs who each reigned for less than one year scores 25 points for naming all three monarchs correctly.
- ■ When checking each other's work, note every error or missing date. Each error carries a penalty of −30 points.
- ■ To finish, total all points for each team and deduct points for errors. The highest total wins MonarchQuest!

Monarch date strips — MonarchQuest

■ Cut into four strips, one per player/team. Ten monarchs are missing from each list.

Date list 1	Date list 2	Date list 3	Date list 4
William I 1066	William I 1066	William I 1066	William I 1066
Edward VI 1547	Edward VI 1547	Edward VI 1547	Edward VI 1547
Henry VII 1485	Henry VII 1485	Henry VII 1485	Henry VII 1485
William and Mary 1689	William and Mary 1689	William and Mary 1689	William and Mary 1689
Jane Grey 1553	Anne 1702	Anne 1702	Anne 1702
Edward VII 1901	James II 1685	James II 1685	James II 1685
Henry V 1413	Edward III 1327	Edward III 1327	Edward III 1327
William IV 1830	Edward VIII 1936	Edward VIII 1936	Edward VIII 1936
George II 1727	Stephen 1135	Stephen 1135	Stephen 1135
Edward IV 1461	Charles II 1660	Charles II 1660	Charles II 1660
Henry I 1100	Edward I 1272	Edward I 1272	Edward I 1272
Charles I 1625	*Oliver Cromwell 1649*	*Oliver Cromwell 1649*	*Oliver Cromwell 1649*
Edward V 1483	Henry III 1216	Henry III 1216	Henry III 1216
Elizabeth II 1952	Edward II 1307	Edward II 1307	Edward II 1307
George III 1760	George III 1760	Jane Grey 1553	Jane Grey 1553
John 1199	John 1199	Edward VII 1901	Edward VII 1901
George VI 1936	George VI 1936	Henry V 1413	Henry V 1413
Henry II 1154	Henry II 1154	William IV 1830	William IV 1830
William III 1694	William III 1694	George II 1727	George II 1727
George I 1714	George I 1714	Edward IV 1461	Edward IV 1461
Elizabeth I 1558	Elizabeth I 1558	Henry I 1100	Henry I 1100
George IV 1820	George IV 1820	Charles I 1625	Charles I 1625
James I 1603	James I 1603	Edward V 1483	Edward V 1483
Richard III 1483	Richard III 1483	Elizabeth II 1952	Elizabeth II 1952
Henry IV 1399	Henry IV 1399	Henry IV 1399	George III 1760
Henry VI 1422	Henry VI 1422	Henry VI 1422	John 1199
Henry VIII 1509	Henry VIII 1509	Henry VIII 1509	George VI 1936
Richard II 1377	Richard II 1377	Richard II 1377	Henry II 1154
George V 1910	George V 1910	George V 1910	William III 1694
William II 1087	William II 1087	William II 1087	George I 1714
Mary I 1553	Mary I 1553	Mary I 1553	Elizabeth I 1558
Richard Cromwell 1658	*Richard Cromwell 1658*	*Richard Cromwell 1658*	George IV 1820
Richard I 1189	Richard I 1189	Richard I 1189	James I 1603
Victoria 1837	Victoria 1837	Victoria 1837	Richard III 1483

REAL-LIFE MATHS   *Ages 9–11 Scenario 1*

NORMANS

1066– _____

1. William I   1066– _____

2.

3.

4.

PLANTAGENETS

1154– _____

1.

3.

4.

5.

6.

7.

8.

HOUSE OF LANCASTER

1399– _____

1.

2.

3.

HOUSE OF YORK

1461– _____

1.

2.

3.

TUDORS

1485– _____

1.

2.

3.

4.

5.

6.

STUARTS

1603– _____

1.

2.

COMMONWEALTH

1649– _____

1.

2.

STUARTS (restored)

1660– _____

1.

2.

3.

4.

5.

HOUSE OF HANOVER
(Georgians and Victorians)

1714– _____

1.

2.

3.

4.

5.

6.

HOUSE OF SAXE-COBURG GOTHA

1901– _____

1.

HOUSE OF WINDSOR

_____ – present

1.

2.

3.

4. Elizabeth II   1952– _____

Teacher notes

Stained-glass designers

Overview
Children must design stained-glass windows to specified requirements, list the amount of materials required and calculate costs.

Timescales
- Lesson 1 (about 1 hour): Introduce children to the scenario and concepts and work through an example.
- Lesson 2 (minimum 1 hour): Children design and cost specific window(s) and list materials.
- Further lessons: Children design and cost a range of windows for multiple commissions.
- Extension: Children devise their own commissions, create scale models and provide costings for the work.

Maths covered
- Understanding shape, calculating areas, measuring, symmetry, scale drawing.
- Calculating costs.
- Clear and logical presentation of work.

Prior learning
Children will need an understanding of area, fractions, scale drawing and multiplication of money.

Cross-curricular links
- Art: creating designs.
- Literacy: speaking and listening.

CD-ROM resources list
- Scenario video and slideshow.
- Photocopiables: Scenario guidelines, Workshop commission lists, Design proposal, Grid paper.

Resource list
Pencils, squared paper, rulers, compasses, protractors, coloured pencils/pens/paper.

Setting the scene
Show children the video and photo slideshow about stained glass on the CD-ROM. Discuss the work needed to make such windows. Explain to the class that they will be taking the role of a highly esteemed design department at a stained-glass workshop. They will receive a range of commissions, and in groups they must organise the work between themselves, producing draft designs and listing materials required. Read the Scenario guidelines together and discuss how groups should try to plan and present their work. If necessary, cover methods for working to scale and calculating simple areas (by calculation or counting squares). If desired, work through a sample commission together.

Running the scenario
Arranging the children in pairs or small groups, give each group a commission from the photocopiable. You may want everyone to have the same commission and then compare work, or you may prefer different groups to have different commissions. Provide copies of the photocopiable Design proposal. Remind children about key factors in planning the window: scale, symmetry, colour schemes, and so on. It will help children to have squared paper available, either $1cm^2$ or $0.5cm^2$; use the Grid paper photocopiable as required. Initially, children should brainstorm ideas, discuss issues and so on. Encourage them to consider carefully the requirements of their specific commission, in particular planning the window to scale before starting on any calculations.

Differentiation
Less confident learners can work only on the design, specifying shapes and features.
More confident learners can develop more complex designs, leading to accurate listings of materials and ultimately costings for the whole window.

Review
Allow children to share their work with each other. Then have one or more groups present to the class. Have groups fulfilled the design commissions they were given? Are children's calculations for material requirements accurate? Is the work clearly presented and easy to understand? Would the clients say yes to their designs?

Further ideas
- Visit local churches and use the internet to look at stained-glass designs.
- Create a commission for your own stained-glass window, either imaginary or for the classroom, and design it.

The stained-glass workshop

Rules for designing and planning

- First and foremost, make sure you give the client what they want!
- Glass pieces can be any shape or size.
- Plan and draw your designs to the required scale on squared paper.
- Assume that the lead has no thickness. (A 1m wide window has ten 10cm pieces of glass across it.)
- There must be a line of lead around the outside of each piece of glass. There must also be a border of lead around the whole design.

Presenting your work

- Draw a scale plan of your proposed window on squared paper. To finish, add thick black lines to represent the lead.
- On your design proposal, say briefly why you think the client will like your work.
- Show your calculations next to your costings.
- Be sure to give an overall cost for your work.

Calculating costs

- Different colours of glass cost different amounts per cm². There is a chart that shows the prices.
- Remember to add the cost of the lead.
- For irregular shapes you may have to estimate the length of lead or the area of glass needed.

Tips for effective working

- Try to look at as many stained-glass windows as possible before you start.
- Start by drawing the outline of your window, and check with your teacher that the scale is correct.
- Try sketching lots of ideas in rough and experiment with different colours.
- Don't waste time colouring in. Save that for your final design, or use coloured paper.
- It is okay to estimate the amount of glass used by counting squares on your design, but you must remember the scale of your drawing. If in doubt, use a formula to calculate area.
- If you are working in a group, make sure that everyone has something to do and that you all agree on your plans.

Straightforward designs	**1.**	**Small square window, 20cm wide by 20cm high** Client would like a chequered pattern, using squares 4cm wide. Scale for design plan = 1:1
	2.	**Small rectangular window, 20cm wide by 40cm high** Repeating pattern wanted, using two colours. Scale for design plan = 1:2
	3.	**Rectangular window, 2.5m wide by 2m high** Different coloured squares wanted, each 10cm long. Must be symmetrical pattern. Scale for design plan = 1:10
	4.	**Large square window, 2m wide by 2m high** Client would like an unusual repeating pattern for the border, surrounding a lovely picture of nature in the centre. Scale for design plan = 1:10
More complex designs	**5.**	**Large square window, 4m wide by 4m high** Client would like an unusual tessellating pattern. Scale for design plan = 1:20
	6.	**A pair of rectangular windows, each 2m wide by 4m high** Windows must be the opposite of each other, in design and colour. Can be abstract or include images of objects. Scale for design plans = 1:20
	7.	**Rectangular window, 2.5m wide by 1.5m high** Must have the word 'HELLO' written in the centre, in glass. Surrounding pattern up to you, but word must stand out. Scale for design plan = 1:10
	8.	**A triangular window, 1m along each side** Client would like all triangles, in a pattern, maybe using the colours of the rainbow. Scale for design plan = 1:5
Open commissions for greater creativity	**9.**	**Two square windows, each 1m high by 1m wide** Client loves sunrises and the moon. Client would like a border for each window too. Scale for design plans = 1:5
	10.	**Arch-like tall window: rectangular (2m wide by 4m high) with semicircle on top** Modern style preferred, representing city life. Scale for design plans = 1:20
	11.	**One circular window, 2m diameter** Symmetrical pattern wanted, radiating from the centre. Use a maximum of four colours. Scale for design plan = 1:10
	12.	**Four small triangular windows, all sides 50cm** Each window must represent a different season of the year, in whatever style you prefer. Scale for design plans = 1:2

Commission

■ Write or stick your commission details here.

■ Describe your design here, and say why you think the client will like it.

■ Show your costing calculations here.

Glass	Cost per 10cm²	Amount used (in cm²)	Total cost
Clear			
Red			
Blue			
Green			
Yellow			
Orange			
Purple			
Pink			
Light yellow			
Light blue			
Light green			
Amount of lead needed at 2p per cm			
		Total cost	

Glass	Clear	Red	Green	Blue	Yellow	Orange	Purple	Pink	Light yellow	Light blue	Light green
Cost per 10cm²	2p	6p	6p	7p	7p	3p	3p	4p	4p	5p	5p

■ Lead costs 2p per cm used. Always round up to the nearest cm.

Decathletes

Overview

Children participate in a virtual decathlon. They monitor their athlete's progress throughout the competition by using simple formulae.

Timescales

- Lesson 1 (1 hour): Introduce the event, the scoring system and formulae. Start the actual decathlon, if time permits.
- Lesson 2 (1 hour): Run the remaining events and then check each other's work. Calculate final scores.
- Repeating Lesson 2: Results change each time you use the *Results generator*. Try reducing the time children have for calculation to add tension.
- Extension: The photocopiable *Decathlon point system* on the CD-ROM contains the actual formulae and parameters used. Children could try repeating the decathlon using these, calculating results either with a calculator or a spreadsheet.

Maths covered

- Using formulae for calculations (including decimals).
- Multiplying up to 1000 and adding up to 10,000.
- Checking work with a calculator.

Prior learning

Children will need an understanding of formulae and the role of brackets in calculations.

Cross-curricular links

- ICT: data handling.
- PE: sport awareness.

CD-ROM resources list

- Scenario video and slideshow.
- On-screen *Results generator*.
- Photocopiables: *Scenario guidelines, Scorecard, Activity sheet, Decathlon point system*.

Resource list

Pencils, paper, calculators.

Setting the scene

Show children the introductory animation on the CD-ROM. Discuss their understanding of the decathlon and explain that they will be taking part in a virtual decathlon, selecting an athlete and monitoring progress. Discuss the photocopiable *Scenario guidelines* and work through a sample calculation for at least one event. Distribute copies of the photocopiable *Scorecard* and talk through how it works, reminding children that they must only complete the first two columns initially.

Running the scenario

Arrange the children individually, in pairs or small groups. Ask children to name their athletes, and then start the decathlon events on your interactive whiteboard. (The photocopiable *Activity sheet* has sample data available if you do not have access to an interactive whiteboard.) Pause after the first event and check that all children understand both how to record the result and calculate their athlete's points for that event. Let the scenario continue to run, giving children challenging time-frames to complete their calculations. Once all ten events have been finished, children check each other's calculations. Children certify whether calculations are correct, or not, and award or deduct additional points appropriately. Once finished, collate all scores and decide on who has come first, second and third.

Differentiation

Less confident learners can ignore the decimal parts of times and distances.
More confident learners could calculate all scores mentally.

Review

Once all work is checked and agreed on, create a final scorecard for all the class to see. Discuss whether children feel the scoring system is fair. (In fact, these simplified formulae are not quite fair.) Do all events have equal status?

Further ideas

Children could plan a decathlon of their own, incorporating events more typical to a primary school. Ask them to devise suitable formulae for each event that give parity between events.

The decathalon

The decathlon is a sporting event for all-round athletes, where they must take part in ten different track and field events over two days. Once a competitor's result is obtained, for example a number of seconds for the 100 metre sprint, a formula is used to calculate the number of points awarded for that event. After ten events, the points are added up and the athlete with the highest total is the winner.

Rules for participating

- You must choose an athlete and stick with them. The results change every time and anyone can win on the day!

- You must use the correct formula for calculating your athlete's points after each event.

- After the last event you must check someone else's work.

- When your calculations are checked, your athlete gains an extra **150** points for every correct calculation, but loses **150** points for every incorrect calculation.

- If you are checking someone's score and you think it is incorrect, you must double-check with them until you agree. Then write down what their score should have been, remembering to deduct **150** points for an incorrect calculation.

Decathlon events

Day 1	Day 2
1. 100 metres (measured in seconds)	**6.** 110 metre hurdles (measured in seconds)
2. Long jump (measured in centimetres)	**7.** Discus throw (measured in metres)
3. Shot put (measured in metres)	**8.** Pole vault (measured in centimetres)
4. High jump (measured in centimetres)	**9.** Javelin throw (measured in metres)
5. 400 metres (measured in seconds)	**10.** 1500 metres (measured in seconds)

Calculating scores

- For track events, score = $A \times (B - P)$
- For jumping and throwing events, score = $A \times (P - B)$
- A and B are parameters that change by event, as shown in the table.
- P is the performance by the athlete, measured in seconds (running), metres (throwing), or centimetres (jumping).
- **Decimals are always ignored in the final score.**

Event	A	B
100m	60	25
Long jump	3	500
Shot put	70	7
High jump	6	75
400m	22	90
110m hurdles	60	28
Discus throw	18	4
Pole vault	2	100
Javelin throw	13	5
1500m	5	410

For example, Athlete 7 runs the 110 metre hurdles in 14.5 seconds. His score will be calculated like this:
Score = $60 \times (28 - 14.5)$, giving 60×13.5, which = 810 points.

Later, for the javelin throw Athlete 7 throws 63.2 metres. His score for this event will be calculated thus:
Score = $13 \times (63.2 - 5)$, giving 13×58.2, which = 756.6, giving 756 points.

Scorecard — Decathletes

Day 1	Time or distance	Score	Checked right or wrong?	+ 150 or − 150 points	Final correct score
100m					
Long jump					
Shot put					
High jump					
400m					

Day 2	Time or distance	Score	Checked right or wrong?	+ 150 or − 150 points	Final correct score
110m hurdles					
Discus throw					
Pole vault					
Javelin throw					
1500m					
				Total points	

■ You must calculate your athlete's score for each event using the following formulae:

Points for track events = A × (B − P)

Points for jumping and throwing events = A × (P − B)

A and B are parameters that vary by event, as shown in the table.

P is the performance by the athlete. It is measured in seconds (running), metres (throwing), or centimetres (jumping).

■ Remember: ignore decimals in the final score.

Event	A	B
100m	60	25
Long jump	3	500
Shot put	70	7
High jump	6	75
400m	22	90
110m hurdles	60	28
Discus throw	18	4
Pole vault	2	100
Javelin throw	13	5
1500m	5	410

- This data has been provided for classes who do not have access to an interactive whiteboard for the lesson. The data below represents results for 12 athletes taking part in a decathlon. It is suggested that each set of data is presented in turn, with enough time allowed for children to calculate their chosen athlete's points.

- Please note that the software on the CD-ROM provides more variety, as all athletes' scores are calculated randomly every time the software is used.

Athletes' results

Event	1	2	3	4	5	6	7	8	9	10	11	12
100m (seconds)	10.77	14.69	12.11	13.69	10.79	13.83	14.73	14.74	12.26	13.86	14.36	12.86
Long jump (centimetres)	712	794	755	776	749	705	743	739	776	785	701	761
Shot put (metres)	18.13	16.24	16.63	17.09	16.09	18.75	16.06	18.47	20.49	20.14	18.30	19.4
High jump (centimetres)	210	182	190	206	205	213	185	214	190	216	221	220
400m (seconds)	56.97	61.50	55.59	61.63	57.81	54.24	59.08	58.38	53.21	61.18	57.11	55.75
110m hurdles (seconds)	17.49	17.99	14.66	17.42	16.52	16.86	14.68	15.93	14.00	13.23	16.89	17.94
Discus throw (metres)	51.16	55.82	43.73	42.99	44.52	51.22	42.56	46.64	44.70	42.50	52.03	44.66
Pole vault (centimetres)	544	545	504	402	486	490	511	468	456	465	516	412
Javelin throw (metres)	64.57	59.36	65.07	70.76	69.41	59.55	61.14	79.30	75.93	60.15	76.17	78.23
1500m (seconds)	252.92	263.67	246.30	232.90	256.54	270.90	261.49	264.66	257.70	264.19	273.21	263.43

Market day

Overview

Children take on the roles of wholesalers, stallholders or customers, buying and selling fruit and vegetables.

Timescales

- Lesson 1 (1 hour): Introduce concepts, consider skills needed, assign roles and prepare for 'market day'.
- Lesson 2 (minimum 1 hour): Run a full 'market day' and evaluate children's work.
- Lesson 3 (minimum 1 hour): Run through 'market day' again, asking children to re-evaluate their approaches to buying and selling. Alternatively, repeat the lesson with children in different roles.
- Extension: Challenge children to research different goods with higher unit prices, such as clothing, and plan a market stall selling those goods at appropriate prices.

Maths covered

- Using appropriate operations.
- Money.

Prior learning

Children will need an understanding of formulae and the role of brackets in calculations.

Cross-curricular links

- Literacy: speaking and listening.
- PSHE: healthy eating, financial awareness.

CD-ROM resources list

- Scenario video and slideshow: wholesale versus public selling; factors involved in pricing goods; choosing foods for a healthy diet.
- Photocopiables: *Scenario guidelines*, *Planning for wholesalers and stallholders*, *Planning for customers*, *Transaction tracking sheet*, cut-out sheets for *Fruit*, *Vegetables* and *Coins*.

Resource list

Pencils, felt pens, paper.

Setting the scene

Watch the introduction on the CD-ROM and discuss the scenario with the class. Explain that they will be taking part in a simulation of Middletown market day. Consider the key skills and factors involved. Model sample interactions from each role's point of view, demonstrating how to track stock, takings and spending. Assign children to roles:

- About half the class should be customers, working on their own or in pairs.
- There should be two or three wholesale distributors. Each wholesaler should have one or two children.
- There should be four to six market stalls. Each stall should have two children.

Distribute the photocopiables *Planning for wholesalers and stallholders* and *Planning for customers*. Ask children to prepare for 'market day': wholesalers choose and price their goods; stallholders decide on their focus, and look at wholesalers' goods; and customers choose the food they want to buy. Food and coins can be cut out from the photocopiables provided on the CD-ROM.

Running the scenario

Arrange the classroom to allow lots of movement. The teacher moderates the 'day' and acts as the farmers, selling more food to the wholesalers as required. (Note that the real value of this activity comes from how children consider and adjust prices as the day unfolds, reflecting competition and demand.) Children should use the *Transaction tracking sheet* from the CD-ROM throughout the task.

Differentiation

Less confident learners should work in pairs, and/or have access to calculation aids.

More confident learners should do all calculations mentally.

Review

At the end of 'market day', allow children ten minutes or so to total their takings or to check their purchases and leftover change using the planning sheets. Who made a good profit? Who spent the least money? What were the most challenging aspects? Would children act differently next time?

Further ideas

- Visit real shops and markets.
- Invite shopkeepers and stallholders to school and interview them. What are the key skills and financial aspects of their work?
- Look at online grocery shopping, and compare websites. What makes companies successful?

- Middletown is famous for its market – the very best quality food, especially the fruit and vegetables. No wonder everyone in Middletown is so healthy!

- You will be assigned one of the following roles:

- a **wholesaler** buying food straight from the farmers and selling it to the stallholders;
- a **stallholder** selling fruit and vegetables at Middletown's market;
- a **member of the public** buying a week's supply of fruit and vegetables for a family of four.

Note: The teacher represents all the farmers, and decides if and when wholesalers can buy more produce.

Rules for 'market day'

Wholesalers

- You start with £200, and you can buy whatever food you wish. The farmers have lots available!

- The prices that you pay the farmers for food are not changeable.

- Will you specialise in certain foods, or have a wide range of fruit and vegetables?

- You can sell food only to stallholders, in any quantity, for example three carrots.

- You can charge stallholders whatever you want for food.

- You must display your prices clearly.

- You can change your prices whenever you want, but not once a transaction has started.

- You cannot discuss and agree on prices with other wholesalers.

- If you run out of food, you can buy more from farmers (the teacher) once the market has started.

Stallholders

- You start with £100. You can buy whatever food you wish as long as the wholesalers have it.

- Will you specialise in certain foods, or have a wide range of fruit and vegetables?

- You can charge members of the public whatever you want for food, with special offers and so on.

- You must display your prices clearly.

- You can change your prices whenever you want, but not once a transaction has started.

- You cannot discuss and agree prices with other stallholders.

- If you run out of food, one of your group can buy more from the wholesalers **if you have enough money** and if they have enough of the food you want.

Members of the public

- You start with £50. You can buy whatever food you wish as long as the stallholders have it.

- You can only buy produce from stallholders.

- You are buying for a household of four people.

- You must buy a range of fruit and vegetables for a varied diet over one week, giving everyone five portions of fruit and vegetables a day.

- If you run out of money, you cannot buy more food, so shop around for the best prices!

Buying and selling rules for everyone

- Keep a note of everything you sell or buy, and how much money you have using the *Transaction tracking sheet.*

- Track all your purchases and sales on paper, including the amount bought/sold and any money spent/received.

- At the end of 'market day', the wholesalers and stallholders calculate their profits or losses. Customers see how much money they have left, and decide whether they had good value for money.

Planning for wholesalers and stallholders

■ **Farmers' prices:** Wholesalers pay these prices to buy food from the farmers.

Fruit

Apples	Kiwis	Pears	Peaches
3p each	4p each	5p each	6p each
Oranges	**Bananas**	**Grapefruit**	**Melons**
7p each	8p each	20p each	30p each

Vegetables

Carrots	Leeks	Onions	Parsnips
5p each	10p each	15p each	20p each
Courgettes	**Cabbages**	**Broccoli**	**Cauliflowers**
25p each	30p each	40p each	50p each

Wholesalers' and stallholders' tracking grids

■ Use these to track your buying and selling.

Fruit	Apples	Kiwis	Pears	Peaches	Oranges	Bananas	Grapefruit	Melons
Quantity bought								
Cost								
Quantity sold								
Income								
Profit or loss								

Veg	Carrots	Leeks	Onions	Parsnips	Courgettes	Cabbages	Broccoli	Cauliflowers
Quantity bought								
Cost								
Quantity sold								
Income								
Profit or loss								

- You are buying for a household of four for a week. You have £50 to spend.

- Each person should have five different portions of fruit and vegetables a day – at least two fruit and at least two vegetables. A single item of any vegetable or fruit counts as one portion, except for **grapefruit, melon, cabbage and cauliflower.** Half of one of these items is a complete portion.

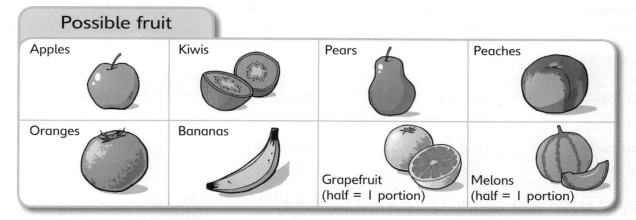

Possible fruit

Apples	Kiwis	Pears	Peaches
Oranges	Bananas	Grapefruit (half = 1 portion)	Melons (half = 1 portion)

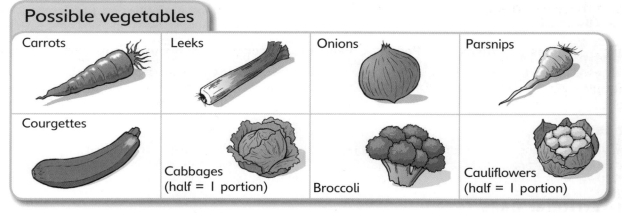

Possible vegetables

Carrots	Leeks	Onions	Parsnips
Courgettes	Cabbages (half = 1 portion)	Broccoli	Cauliflowers (half = 1 portion)

Customer's planning grid

- Use this to plan the week's fruit and vegetables. You can only buy produce from stallholders.

Day	Remember: five fruit and vegetables needed **per person** each day
Monday	
Tuesday	
Wednesday	
Thursday	
Friday	
Saturday	
Sunday	

In the gym

Overview

Children create appropriate exercise programmes for new gym members, and then predict their progress over a period of time.

Timescales

- Lesson 1 (1 hour): Introduce children to the scenario and concepts, and work through an example.
- Lesson 2 (1 hour): Children prepare an exercise plan for one new member, and predict their progress.
- Further lessons: Children design and monitor exercise programmes for a range of new members.
- Extension: Children use formulae to calculate the body mass index (BMI); research nutrition; and research the effect of exercise on heart rate.

Maths covered

- Reading charts.
- Approximating and estimating.
- Adding and subtracting up to HTU.
- Clear and logical presentation of work.

Prior learning

Children will need an understanding of charts and graphs, and adding and subtracting up to HTU.

Cross-curricular links

- Science, PE and PSHE: healthy living and the functioning of the heart and body.

CD-ROM resources list

- Scenario video and slideshow.
- Photocopiables: Scenario guidelines, New members sheet, Member monitoring form, BMI chart, Heart rates chart, Exercise chart, Helpful links for teachers.

Resource list

Pencils, paper, charts for display on interactive whiteboard (if available).

Setting the scene

Show children the video and photo slideshow on the CD-ROM. Discuss exercise and nutrition. Explain to the class that they will take the role of gym instructors. They will work with a range of new members. Each has different needs, but all desire to be healthier and fitter. Talk through the photocopiable *Scenario guidelines*, the charts on the photocopiables on the CD-ROM and how to use them. Work through a sample programme together. Stress that although nutrition is not mentioned here, it plays a large part in our health. Children should assume that all new members eat a healthy diet.

Running the scenario

Arrange children individually, in pairs or small groups. Provide the photocopiables *Scenario guidelines* and *Member monitoring form*. Assign a new gym member to each group. (All groups might have the same person and then compare exercise programmes, or different groups could have different people.) Encourage children to brainstorm ideas, discuss issues, and to consider carefully the requirements of their specific person. Remind them about key factors in planning an exercise regime: age, weight, fitness level and objectives. Stress that their exercise programmes must not overexert their person. People who are unfit should have gentle exercises until they have improved sufficiently, however long that takes.

Differentiation

Less confident learners may need support in estimating and calculating calories burned.

More confident learners can plan a further six months in detail, with different/harder exercises. They could also represent progress graphically.

Review

Ask one or more groups to present to the class. Have groups fulfilled the needs of their assigned people? Are children's predictions accurate? Would the people be pleased with their programmes? Would this be useful in real life?

Further ideas

- Try drawing graphs to show monthly changes.
- Investigate dietary changes and how these affect weight loss and health too.

Welcome to the gym, where you take the role of a fitness instructor devising exercise programmes for new members.

■ You will need:
- a body mass index chart
- a heart rates chart
- an exercise chart

Creating exercise programmes

- Assume that all people will have a healthy, balanced diet, and that the rest of their daily activity will be the same as usual.
- To be effective, exercise programmes must be appropriate for the person doing them. This is affected by their age, their BMI, and their current level of fitness.
- Exercises must be varied to keep people keen, but you must not overexert anyone.
- Use the exercise chart to assign exercises for people and calculate calories used.

Estimating fitness

- You must start by assessing body mass index (BMI) and heart rate when resting. Usually, the higher a person's BMI and heart rate, the less they can exert themselves. They may need gentler exercises at first.

Estimating fitness changes

- Assume that if people burn up to 500 calories **per workout** they will lose about 1kg **per month**, if they burn 500 to 1000 calories per workout they will lose 2kg per month, and so on.
- Also, assume that for every month of exercise a person's resting heart rate improves by two beats per minute.

Predicting progress

- Change exercises each month as appropriate and predict progress month by month.
- Suggest what changes could happen over a year with continued exercise.
- **Note:** When someone reaches a healthy weight, assume that they will adjust their diet to **maintain** that weight, though their fitness can continue to improve.

Name	Objectives	Age	Height (m)	Weight (kg)	Resting heart rate (beats per minute)
John Thompson	John hasn't exercised for a long time. He wants to lose weight and become fitter now he has retired.	62	1.73	92	85
Zulekha Sarween	Zulekha loves aerobics, and wants to improve her general fitness.	37	1.57	69	74
Andrea Simpson	Andrea uses a wheelchair. She wants to improve her upper body strength, lose weight and get fitter. (Apart from the running machine and gym ball, all equipment can be modified for wheelchair users.)	55	1.83	84	82
Hameed Khan	Hameed wants to stay as mobile and as healthy as possible. He has a bad knee and so he can't use the running or cycling machines.	80	1.80	82	72
Joanne James	Joanne wants to get ready for a half marathon in six months' time!	23	1.62	69	69
Den Chin	Den loves rowing. He wants to get really fit and then start competing in rowing races.	18	1.70	73	70

Sample exercise plan

Fitness plan for: *Albert Scuttle*	
Age	54
Height	1.57m
Weight	82kg
BMI	33 (overweight)
Resting heart rate	85 (poor)

Describe the programme here:

We have given Albert a good mixture of exercises to keep him motivated. Because he hasn't done any exercise for some time, his programme at the gym starts very gently and gets a little bit harder as the weeks progress.

We would recommend that he continues coming to the gym after the six months are up. If he does, then he will see more improvements.

Month 1

Exercises: 60-minute plan to be completed three times a week				Weight loss	Heart rate change (beats per minute)
Warm up	Stretching	10 mins	45 calories	417 calories per workout = 1kg	−2
Exercise 1	Rowing machine: slow	20 mins	160 calories		
Exercise 2	Gentle aerobics	20 mins	160 calories		
Exercise 3	Weightlifting: light	5 mins	22 calories		
Cool down	Gym ball exercises	5 mins	30 calories		

Member monitoring form — In the gym

Fitness plan for:	
Age	
Height	
Weight	
BMI	
Resting heart rate	

■ Describe the programme here:

Month	Exercises: 60-minute plan to be completed three times a week	Weight loss	Heart rate change (beats per minute)
1			
2			
3			
4			
5			
6			

■ Predictions for after six months:

New weight:	New BMI:	New resting heart rate:

■ Write suggestions overleaf for how this member might improve if they continue for a further six months. Could they do more strenuous exercises?

Teacher notes

Beautiful bathrooms

Overview

Using price lists and plans, children have to design and cost a range of bathrooms to fit different customers' needs.

Timescales

- Lesson 1 (about 1 hour): Introduce concepts; consider skills needed and approaches to presenting work.
- Lesson 2 (minimum 1 hour): Children design and cost a bathroom for a specific customer.
- Further lessons (minimum 1 hour): Children design bathrooms for other customers, using given data or actual items researched from the internet.
- Extension: Children calculate completed estimates for all customers, including profit margins and labour costs, and estimate overall profits for the business over a period of time.

Maths covered

- Using appropriate operations.
- Adding (using pencil and paper or calculator) several amounts of money to over £1000.
- Calculating areas.
- Clear and logical presentation of work.

Prior learning

Children should be familiar with calculating areas and calculating using money.

Cross-curricular links

- D&T: design.
- PSHE: financial awareness.

CD-ROM resources list

- Scenario video and slideshow.
- Sample costing and design.
- Sample estimate.
- Photocopiables: *Scenario guidelines, Bathroom supplies price list, Customer profiles.*

Resource list

Pencils, paper, rulers, calculators (optional).

Setting the scene

Explain to the class that their task is to redesign one or more bathrooms for Dave Diamond's demanding customers to suit their needs and budget. Briefly discuss the key features

and requirements of a bathroom. Then open the CD-ROM on your interactive whiteboard to let the children meet Dave and see different bathrooms. Discuss key features to help give children a broad range of ideas. Introduce one or more of the customers, and then finish by looking together at the photocopiables *Scenario guidelines* and *Bathroom supplies price list.* Discuss, model and review the different maths skills involved and how to record their work.

Running the scenario

Arrange children individually, in pairs, or small groups and give each group photocopiables *Bathroom supplies price list* and *Customer profiles.* (Every group could have the same customer, and then compare ideas, or different groups might have different customers.) Ensure the *Scenario guidelines* are available, either on the interactive whiteboard or as a photocopiable per group. Encourage children to consider carefully their customer's requirements before starting their calculations. Remind children of the importance of the layout of their work – both design and showing costs.

Differentiation:

Less confident learners might consider only bathroom furniture, not the tiling, painting or flooring.
More confident learners can use the 'person-power chart' to include profits and estimate labour costs.

Review

Allow children to share their work with each other, and then have one or more groups pitch/present to the class. Are the children's calculations accurate? Is the work clearly presented and easy to understand? What would Dave Diamond think? Will the customers be happy?

Further ideas

- Use catalogues and websites to look at real bathroom supplies and design your own bathroom, either imaginary or for home.
- Why not move on to kitchens? Dave Diamond would be most interested in new ideas for expanding his business.

Dave Diamond

Dave is the owner of Beautiful Bathrooms, which he founded ten years ago. The company provides great bathrooms that suit people's needs and personalities, whatever their budget!

He has four new customers who all want a new bathroom. Dave wants you, his new design team, to come up with the right bathroom for the right customer, and to tell him how much it will cost.

You must remember that this is how much it will cost Dave to buy all the parts from his supplier. He always adds on a percentage for his own profits. Of course, he has to charge for the person-power to do the work. How else would you get paid?

Rules for designing and planning

- First and foremost, make sure you give the customers what they want!

- All rooms are 3m high.

- All sinks are 40cm wide, 50cm deep and 75cm high.

- All bathtubs are 200cm long, 70cm wide and 50cm high.

- All showers have a 1m² base and are 2.5m high.

- All toilets are 55cm deep, 35cm wide and 75cm high.

- Showers must go in a corner, and must have tiles behind them.

- Toilets must go against a wall and have 1m² of free floor area around them.

- You must not put flooring under a shower.

- Toilets and baths do not have to have tiles behind them otherwise you can put tiles anywhere you want.

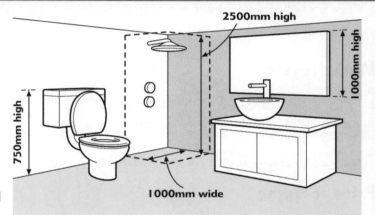

- Tiles do not have to go higher than 40cm above the top of a sink, bath or shower.

- Ceilings should only be painted.

- All doors are 1m wide and 2m high, and must be painted.

- Don't worry about windows or lights. They will be sorted out separately.

Presenting your work

- Draw a plan of your proposed bathroom layout: a separate plan for each wall and the floor.

- Show all calculations neatly in separate areas.

- You must show an overall cost for all the equipment and materials.

Calculating profits and labour costs

- If you move on to preparing the actual customer estimates, Dave simply adds 10% on to all costs. To calculate costs of workers to fit the bathroom, use the information about person-power. Remember that profit for Dave does not include his staff's wages.

Bathroom supplies price list — Beautiful bathrooms

Sinks (All sinks are 75cm high, 40cm wide and 50cm deep.)

Happy washer
Recycled glass, basic taps, £55

Pure style
White with chrome taps, £99

Rock star
Solid glass, gold-plated taps, £147

Unlimited luxury
Hand-styled porcelain, £225

Bathtubs (All bathtubs are 200cm long, 50cm high and 70cm wide.)

Rub-a-dub-dub
Basic shape, basic taps, £125

Sleek-soaker
Elegant shape, snazzy taps, £199

Beauty-bather
Built-in headrest, gold-plated taps, £347

Pearl-in-the-shell
Shell-shaped, built-in bubble machine, £825

Showers (All showers have a 1m² base and are 2.5m high.)

5-minute wonder
Clear glass, basic controls, £145

Downpour
Clear glass, huge showerhead, £211

Waterfall
Patterned glass, plays soothing music, £375

Jet massage
Multi-spray for all round cleaning, £599

Toilets (All toilets are 75cm high, 55cm deep and 35cm wide.)

Flush 'n' go
Recycled glass, no fuss, £65

Comfort
Heated seat with fur top, £149

Soothing sounds
Plays music when used, £299

Silent swish
Works entirely by sensors, £315

Wall tiles (All tiles are 20cm by 20cm.)

White 'n' simple	Chequered (choice of colours)	Sleek silver	Glittering gold
25p per tile	40p per tile	65p per tile	£1 per tile

Flooring

Basic lino	Cork	Solid oak	Polished marble
£13 per m²	£21 per m²	£32 per m²	£45 per m²

Paints

Prices are per litre.
One litre covers 1m².

Pure white: £15 per litre.
All other colours: £18 per litre.

Extras

Mirrors (1m × 50cm)

Basic	£9
Stylish	£18
Delux	£32
Posh (full length)	£95

Cabinets (40cm wide, 50cm high and 30cm deep)

Basic	£12
Stylish	£23
Delux	£40
Posh (inside lighting)	£70

Bath mats

Basic	£8
Stylish	£17
Delux	£29
Posh (foot massage)	£52

Towel racks (fixed onto tiles/painted wall)

Basic	£10
Stylish	£17
Delux	£31
Posh (heated)	£85

Loo-roll holders (10cm × 10cm)

Basic	£4
Stylish	£11
Delux	£19
Posh (motorised)	£34

Waste bins

Basic	£8
Stylish	£14
Delux	£21
Posh (musical)	£48

Person-power, times and costs

Dave charges customers £30 per hour worked per person, and pays his workers £15 per hour.

Fitting sink: 2hrs	**Fitting bath: 3hrs**	**Fitting shower: 4hrs**	**Fitting toilet: 3hrs**
Painting: 30mins per m²	**Tiling: 2hrs per m²**	**Laying floor: 1hr per m²**	**Fitting extras: 15mins per item**

Angela Jolly

Darling, with a reputation like mine you simply have to have a bit of luxury in your life. There are only me and Charlie, my cutesie little doggie, but I want the best, the best!

I want the largest bath possible right in the middle of the room. I also want a space for little Charlie to have a basket so he can snooze while I soak in luxury! Oh, and I don't need a toilet – I have a separate one already darling!

5m

6m

Existing toilet 2m×2m

1.5m

0.5m

Harold Bucket

I'm a straightforward sort of chap with no interest in bathrooms at all. As long as I can clean myself, I don't care.

I live alone and have a tiny bathroom. If the price is right I'll say yes. (In other words, I want it as cheap as possible!)

And by the way, I hate white walls.

3m

1m

2m

Johnny Zigzag

Being a rock star I ain't too bothered about being clean and all man, but I do like to impress my guests at parties.

And guess what, I've got a bit of a strange-shaped bathroom. It's all 'cos of the separate loo, so I don't need one of those, man. Keep it to yerself man, but even though I'm famous, I ain't got too much cash. So don't go too over the top man!

1.5m

5m

Existing toilet 2m×2m

0.5m

5m

The Walton Family

There are six of us, and life is crazy! You can imagine us in the mornings: getting people off to work and school, and little baby William is still only one year old! Luckily we have a **huge** bathroom, so we definitely want two sinks, two loos, a shower **and** a bath. Not too expensive though, but please do try to give the place a nice cosy feel to it.

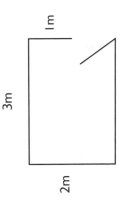

6m

8m

5m

Global city-dash 3000

Overview

Children race around the globe in space-age jets, visiting each continent once, stopping in a capital city of their choice.

Timescales

- Lesson I (about I hour): Introduce the event and the concepts. Work in small groups to plan a strategy and route.
- Lesson 2 (minimum I hour): Run the race and check workings.
- Repeating Lesson 2: Repeat the race, either at a harder level, or using different starting points or routes.
- Extension: Use maps on the internet and other online tools for planning other races.

Maths covered

- Calculating distances using larger numbers.
- Time (24-hour clock), including calculating minutes from decimals.
- Approximating.
- Reading charts.

Prior learning

Children should have an awareness of time zones, and the ability to use larger numbers with the four operations.

Cross-curricular links

- Geography: awareness of world geography.
- Literacy: speaking and listening.

CD-ROM resources list

- Scenario video and slideshow.
- Photocopiables: *Scenario guidelines, Mileage chart, Race recording sheet, Time zone chart, Time zone map, Target city map.*

Resource list

Pencils, paper, rulers, calculators (optional, but advisable), maps and globes (optional).

Setting the scene

Check children's understanding of continents and capital cities. Also discuss time zones and how they relate to Greenwich Mean Time (GMT) (refer to the *Time zone map* on an interactive whiteboard). Show the introductory video on the CD-ROM, and explain that children will compete in the latest Global city-dash 3000. Display or distribute the photocopiables *Scenario guidelines* and *Target city map*. Explain the rules of the competition and the attributes of each jet. Stress that racers must stop in every continent (except Antarctica), at any one of the capital cities given for each continent. Children could all start from the same city, or choose their own starting point.

Running the scenario

In Lesson I, arrange children in pairs or small groups. Give each group the photocopiables *Mileage chart, Time zone chart* and *Race recording sheet.* Talk through a sample journey to demonstrate planning and recording. Stress the need for estimation when planning, rather than carrying out exact calculations. For the actual race, where exact calculations are required, you can add tension by setting time intervals for each stage of the journey. Calculators are advisable, and it is imperative that children check each other's work using them.

Differentiation

Note that different levels of race are specified in the *Scenario guidelines.*
Less confident learners might work only on the route, specifying distances travelled between locations and the overall distance travelled.
More confident learners should bear in mind time zones and fuel requirements. They should refer to the *Time zone map* or *Time zone chart.*

Review

Once the winners have been established, discuss difficulties, tactics and useful points. Could children improve on their times for the next race?

Further ideas

With appropriate information and resources to hand, this activity is repeatable in many ways, such as travel the world stopping at ten cities beginning with the letter B, or visit six famous tourist attractions in as fast a time as possible.

Global city-dash 3000 annual challenge

■ The year is 3270. The world has changed beyond our wildest dreams. The latest jets, powered by non-polluting fuels, are fast and can stop in an instant. Since the new millennium in the year 3000, competitors have taken part in the Global city-dash 3000. This is a race to travel around the globe. This year **you** are in the race!

Rules

● You must stop at one city per continent, in any order you want to, and finish in the same city you started from – as quickly as possible!

● The race starts at noon GMT (that is, 1200 hours in London).

● For the harder races, you cannot fly to a city if you do not have enough fuel to get there.

Standard race

Everyone uses the same jet, with no fuel limits. (Feather is the easiest for time calculations.)

Harder race

Choose your jet from the three available. Refuelling adds 15 minutes onto a stop.

All jets hold 100 gallons of fuel, but the faster they are, the fewer miles they do per gallon. This means that they cannot fly as far per gallon.

You may stop at more than one city in a continent if you need to refuel, but you do not have to.

Super-hard race

As for the harder race, but only the thunderbolt jet is available.

In all cities, refuelling depots are closed from midnight until 9am, **local time**. If they are shut when you arrive, then you must wait until they reopen.

Mind-bender race

Visit all 24 cities in any order you wish, monitoring fuel and time.

Travel-craft available

● All jets hold 100 gallons of etho-pure non-polluting fuel.

● All refuelling stations are only open between 9am and 9pm local time.

Jet	Description	Miles per gallon	Average speed
Feather	Lightweight and economical	120	1000 miles per hour
Focus	A good all-rounder	100	1100 miles per hour
Thunderbolt	Solid and fast	80	1200 miles per hour

Tips for calculating times and fuel requirements

● Journey time = distance divided by speed. ● Fuel used = distance divided by miles per gallon.

● To convert decimal times to minutes, multiply the decimal of the time by 60. For example, 1.5 hours = 1 hour 30 minutes.

● Arrival times: remember to adjust to local time in the harder games.

Mileage chart – Global city-dash 3000

■ To find the distance between two cities, find the name of one city on the left of the chart, and the other at the bottom.

■ All destinations have been rounded to the nearest mile.

	Abuja	Addis Ababa	Kigali	Pretoria	Beijing	New Delhi	Moscow	Tokyo	Budapest	London	Reykjavik	Rome	Agana	Apia	Canberra	Wellington	Havana	Mexico City	Ottawa	Washington DC	Brasilia	Buenos Aires	Caracas	Lima
Abuja	-----																							
Addis Ababa	2135	-----																						
Kigali	1732	967	-----																					
Pretoria	2781	2508	1651	-----																				
Beijing	6801	5173	6118	7256	-----																			
New Delhi	5499	2842	3773	4976	2350	-----																		
Moscow	3621	3233	4014	5665	3604	2701	-----																	
Tokyo	8062	6467	7402	8400	1302	3630	4652	-----																
Budapest	2744	2901	3485	5098	4566	3337	976	5627	-----															
London	2967	3668	4099	5614	5065	4174	1556	5947	901	-----														
Reykjavik	4072	4798	5273	6777	4904	4721	2056	5473	1910	1174	-----													
Rome	2292	2780	3227	4785	5055	3681	1478	6130	504	891	2052	-----												
Agana	9128	7138	7917	8268	2510	4429	6101	1568	7071	7486	7036	7564	-----											
Apia	12,117	10,358	10,599	9402	5913	7945	9156	4670	10040	9804	8684	10493	3528	-----										
Canberra	9428	7733	7756	6731	5603	6441	9008	4947	9777	10,564	10,419	10,088	3385	2841	-----									
Wellington	10,090	8965	8729	7343	6706	7869	10,294	5771	11,183	11,704	10,735	11,535	4246	2065	1447	-----								
Havana	5961	7890	7702	8126	7925	8620	5963	7539	5561	4660	3911	5409	8379	6557	9267	7913	-----							
Mexico City	7080	8971	8810	9079	7750	9117	6668	7034	6446	5555	4637	6370	7543	5447	8197	6907	1110	-----						
Ottawa	5450	6923	7083	8125	6501	7052	4453	6420	4214	3335	2403	4186	7657	7192	10,020	9010	1587	2242	-----					
Washington DC	5540	7169	7227	8106	6934	7493	4866	6783	4563	3669	2810	4489	7934	7070	9918	8760	1135	1886	457	-----				
Brasilia	4161	6172	5388	4909	10,539	8857	6951	10,801	6097	5505	5649	5639	11,587	8096	8758	7589	3560	4250	4577	4018	-----			
Buenos Aires	5253	6982	6060	5054	11,985	9824	8383	11,428	7423	6922	7114	6936	10,395	8015	7300	6210	4294	4598	5641	5223	1466	-----		
Caracas	5059	7159	6723	6853	8958	8835	6178	8815	5503	4663	4299	5197	9718	7593	9613	8168	1344	2236	2472	2062	2235	3170	-----	
Lima	5992	8089	7351	6784	10,359	10,341	7868	9639	7123	6329	6006	6758	9633	6852	7995	6586	2463	2649	3979	3527	1698	1950	1711	-----

Race recording sheet — Global city-dash 3000

Name(s): _____   Race level: _____

Jet: _____   Miles per gallon: _____   Average speed: _____ miles per hour

Starting city: _____   Starting time (local time): _____ (12 noon in London)

Note: The standard race uses only the Feather Jet, and there are no fuel requirements.

Race planning chart

■ Use this chart to estimate your race details.

■ Tip for estimating: approximate to the nearest 10 or 15 minutes.

Stage	From	To	Miles travelled	Approx. flight time	Approx. local time arrived	Approx. fuel used	Refuel?
1							
2							
3							
4							
5							
Finishing point							

Race grid

■ Use this chart to show accurate race details.

Stage	From	To	Miles travelled	Flight time	Exact local time arrived	Refuel?	Exact departure time (local)
1							
2							
3							
4							
5							
Finishing point							

Exact time taken = _____

A world of statistics

Overview
Children interpret a report containing a range of information and present their findings in meaningful ways.

Timescales
- Lesson 1 (minimum 1 hour): Introduce the concepts, read the report and children plan their presentation.
- Lesson 2 (minimum 1 hour): Children must prepare and deliver their presentations.
- Lesson 3 (about 1 hour): Children deliver and discuss their presentations.
- Extension: Children could conduct further research, ideally online, into their chosen countries of focus.

Maths covered
- Using and rounding larger numbers.
- Percentages and fractions.
- Data handling and interpretation.

Prior learning
An understanding of graphs and charts is needed; an ability to calculate percentages would be useful.

Cross-curricular links
- Literacy: speaking and listening.
- Geography: global understanding.
- ICT: data handling.

CD-ROM resources list
- Scenario video and slideshow.
- Photocopiables: *Scenario guidelines, The report, Presentation plan, Useful statistics links.*
- Data handling tools: tables, line graphs, bar graphs, pie charts.

Resource list
Pencils, paper, atlases, globes, calculators (optional), ICT suite with internet access (optional).

Setting the scene
Explain to the class that they will be learning how data is used to help us understand more about how the world is changing. They will be reading a report containing a range of information about certain countries in the world, and their task will be to interpret the information and create an informative, easy-to-digest presentation from it. Initially, spend some time working through the *Scenario guidelines* with the whole class. Ensure that children understand what is meant by 'statistics', and that they appreciate the use of graphs and charts to help visualise information. Also, try to cover rounding numbers, and working in units of millions (for example, 1.5 million).

Running the scenario
Arrange the children individually, in pairs or small groups as desired. Distribute or display the *Scenario guidelines*, and give one copy of the photocopiables *The report* and *Presentation plan* to each group. In Lesson 1, stress that children should focus on planning their presentation. It is essential that children have plenty of time to consider the data available and what it might mean. For creating and delivering the presentation, use your discretion as to whether children work with the computer (there are a range of data handling tools on the CD-ROM) or on paper.

Differentiation
Conclusions in children's presentations are largely differentiated by outcome.
Less confident learners should round numbers to make them more manageable, and produce simpler charts or use calculators to assist their calculations.
More confident learners should consider the use of pie charts for presenting some information, and could try to collate further facts if time permits.

Review
In reviewing work, consider whether children are able to represent data appropriately. In particular, look for meaningful deductions and ideas about what the data suggests.

Further ideas
Use the *Useful statistics links* sheet to investigate data for other countries.

Scenario guidelines — A world of statistics

What is 'statistics'?

Statistics is the collection, organisation, analysis, and interpretation of data. Statistics usually consists of sets of numbers. They can be understood more easily by using different charts and graphs. People can use the information in these charts and graphs to draw conclusions.

For example, a chart that many people know is a football league table. This contains data about each team (such as games won, goals scored, and so on). The data is most easily understood in a simple table (see below). In this case, the total points are in descending order. However, when the numbers become more complicated, or there is a lot more information, people often use more visual techniques, such as bar charts. These help people to see quickly what is going on.

Global statistics

With the revolution of technology that has happened in the last 50 years, more and more data is being collected about more and more of the world. This provides information about how the world is changing. Not everyone agrees that all the information is correct. It is true that collecting accurate numbers is very hard, but the use of data to report on the world is a fact that is here to stay. How useful this is all depends on how it is used!

Presenting information

Tables are great for presenting numbers.

Position	Team	Played	Goal difference	Points
1	Newcastle	25	+ 45	65
2	Liverpool	26	+ 40	64
3	Man U	25	+ 33	60
4	Man C	24	+ 32	58
5	Bolton	26	+ 20	50
6	Wigan	25	+ 25	48
7=	Everton	24	+ 18	42
7=	Sunderland	25	+ 2	42

Line graphs are useful for showing how things change over time.

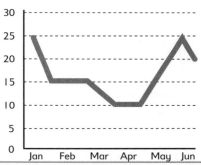

Bar charts are great for comparing amounts.

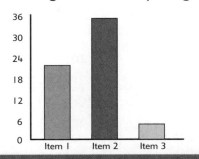

Pie charts are great for showing percentages and fractions.

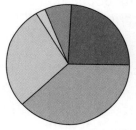

Using information

More important than showing the information, is what you learn from it. It is up to you what facts you try to deduce. As you read the report, think about what you want to try to learn from the data.

It is amazing to think that 200 years ago, the population of the world was only around 1 billion. (A billion is a thousand million.) It reached 2 billion around 1930 and 3 billion in 1960. It then increased by 1 billion roughly every 13 years, reaching a mind-boggling 7 billion in 2012. Some experts believe that it may reach an estimated 10–15 billion people by around 2090. No one is quite sure when the population will stop growing. Some people think it won't get much higher than 10 billion, but nobody knows for sure. Advances in medicine and the supply of food and water help people to live longer. However, 1 in 12 people still don't have access to clean water, and diseases, famines and natural disasters can have terrible consequences for many.

Better living conditions can mean that people live longer, so populations can grow and people can move around more. With the development of high-speed travel and the internet, more and more people are travelling around the world for leisure or work, and many people have easy access to all sorts of information. This is changing the world in a way that is referred to as **globalisation**.

Not all of the world develops at the same time. Countries like the United Kingdom have developed over hundreds of years and are rich, whereas some countries have many problems. China is the fastest growing country at the moment. This means that it is becoming richer faster than any other country.

We compared six very different countries around the world to see just how things have changed, and to consider what the future might hold for them, and the rest of the world. Here is some data about each place:

Country	Continent	Approximate area (million km²)	Population in 2011	Approximate GDP per person in 2010 (US $)	Potatoes produced in 2010 (tonnes)	Electricity used per person in 2008 (kwh)
China	Asia (Far East)	9.6	1,347,565,324	$7,700	74,799,084	2,789
Egypt	Africa (North)	1.0	82,536,770	$6,500	3,643,220	1,322
Guatemala	Central America	0.11	14,757,316	$5,000	472,600	482
New Zealand	Oceania	0.25	4,414,509	$27,900	531,100	8,840
UK	Europe	0.25	62,417,431	$35,900	6,045,000	5,522
World		(land)148.94	6,974,036,375	$11,500	324,181,889	2601

Look how the population of each of these countries has changed since 1950, and how they may have changed by 2100.

Country	1950	2009	2015	2025	2050	2100
China	544,950,886	1,345,750,973	1,395,998,248	1,453,140,188	1,417,044,807	941,042,001
Egypt	21,514,024	82,999,393	91,778,427	104,970,055	129,533,301	123,227,316
Guatemala	3,146,073	14,026,947	16,226,517	19,926,808	27,480,325	45, 753,000
New Zealand	1,908,001	4,266,498	4,491,783	4,831,018	5,348,528	6,323,000
UK	50,615,999	61,565,422	63,527,927	66,600,777	72,365,492	75,676,046
World population	2,537,326,718	6,852,310,438	7,325,986,263	8,035,833,231	9,173,384,240	10,124,926,196

These figures scare some people. For others they present a challenge. Either way, although global statistics are hard to collect accurately, what these numbers do tell us is that the world is going to be a very different place in 100 years' time. What do you think?

Your task: Create an interesting presentation using some of the data in the report. Use this sheet to plan your presentation. Before you start, here are some helpful guidelines.

About the data

- Data about countries is hard to collect accurately. You may find data in other places that is different from the report you have read.

- Remember that some of the data is in millions, so where the area of the UK is listed as 0.25 million km², that means 250,000km². The main thing is to use the numbers to compare different countries.

- It is okay to round numbers if you are calculating using mental or pencil and paper methods.

- **GDP** means gross domestic product *per person*. It is how much 'wealth' is produced per person in each country in a year.

Tips for a strong presentation

- Decide whether you will focus on one country, or maybe compare two countries in different ways, or perhaps compare all five countries for one or two things.

- Will you use paper or ICT? (Both have advantages and disadvantages.)

- Try to finish your presentation with some interesting conclusions. Can you suggest what might happen even further into the future, for the world or for particular countries?

Your focus

Write here what you want your report to be about:

Information we will need

Note here the data you will need:

Our presentation

Write here how you intend to lay out your presentation including what charts you will prepare, and how you might deliver it to the rest of the class:

Four-a-side football

Overview

Groups participate in an auction to build a four-a-side football team. They then play in a mini-league, using probability to decide events.

Timescales

- Lesson 1 (about 1 hour): Introduce the concepts and work through examples. Hold the player auction.
- Lesson 2 (minimum 1 hour): Demonstrate gameplay, run the league, collate results and find the champions.
- Lesson 3 (about 1 hour): If you have asked children to track their individual players' performances (saves made versus goals conceded and so on), over all their games, analyse the results. Do the players' original odds match their statistical rating? If there were to be a new auction, how would you change a player's worth and rating?
- Extension: Allow children to devise their own player probability charts, using different criteria to rate probability odds (such as a pack of cards, coins).

Maths covered

- Adding numbers with one decimal place up to 10.
- Probability.

Prior learning

Children will need a basic understanding of probability and an ability to calculate with decimals.

Cross-curricular links

- Literacy: speaking and listening.
- ICT: data handling.
- PE: sport awareness.

CD-ROM resources list

- Scenario video and slideshow.
- Photocopiables: *Scenario guidelines, Player lists for auction, Team results sheet, Pitch plan, Typical gameplay, Our league table.*

Resource list

Pencils, dice, coins, counters, whistle (optional).

Setting the scene

Show children the introductory animation on the CD-ROM and the photocopiable *Player lists for auction*. Discuss the auction process and the rules of the game. If necessary, explain the probability concepts that children will need. Ideally, there should be eight teams, with a maximum of four children in a team. (If some groups only have three members, one member should take responsibility for two players.) Give children time to study the different players for each position and plan their strategy.

Running the scenario

The teacher organises and runs the player auction. (You may prefer children to compile their own teams and ignore player overlaps.) You need a fair bidding process and a secure way of monitoring how much each team has spent of its six million pounds. Provide each team with a copy of the *Team results sheet, Pitch plan* and *Typical gameplay*. Carry out a whole-class demonstration game. Remind children that the teacher's decision is final: when the whistle goes, the game ends, even mid-roll! Plan a system of rotation so that every team plays each other once. Remember to ask children to track players' performances if you are going to sustain the focus on probability (see Lesson 3 above).

Differentiation

Less confident learners should monitor the strikers as they have fewer functions.

More confident learners should monitor all of the data generated by their team for each game.

Review

Once a final league table has been created (using *Our league table*), discuss whether children think the rules are fair. Would they change them? How might they improve the game?

Further ideas

Teams can negotiate player transfers with each other before the new season starts. They could also set up an actual fantasy league for your class.

Scenario guidelines — Four-a-side football

Rules for the auction

- The teacher will run the auction to ensure fairness.

- Each group has a budget of £6 million to buy four players. You cannot spend more. If you spend too much at first, you may have to play with three players. If you have money left over, you cannot use it.

- Think about your tactics before the auction, and spend wisely!

Rules for the league

- Every team must play each other once:

Win = 3 points, Draw = 1 point, Loss = 0 points

- Try to track players' actions during each game.

- At the end of a game, both teams must note the score and their own goal difference. Then calculate total goal difference and total points so far, before moving on to the next game.

- After all games, the team with the most points wins the league. Goal difference decides ties.

■ Lay out your teams on a pitch plan.

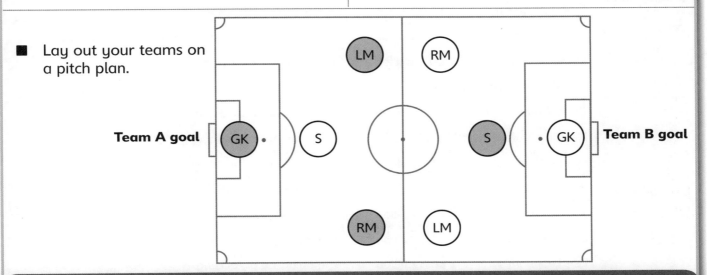

Rules for matches

- To begin, colour-in and cut out your counters and position your 'players' on a pitch plan. Use the counters to show who has the ball.

- Each game lasts 5 minutes, with no half-time.

- Toss a coin or roll the dice to see who starts. This is 'TEAM A'. The ball always starts with the goalkeeper of TEAM A.

- When a goalkeeper passes to a midfielder, the other team's midfielder has a chance to tackle. If they succeed, they get the ball and can pass immediately.

- After a team shoots (whether they have scored a goal or not) the ball restarts with the other team's goalkeeper.

- Whenever a player is going to roll the dice they **must** state their probability of being successful in advance (according to their key skills) and state what number(s) they want to roll. Once the other team agrees with the chosen number(s), the dice can be rolled.

- Players must not move around the pitch.

- **Goalkeepers can**:
    - Pass to midfielders
    - Shoot (roll a dice and toss a coin)
    - Save the other team's shots (roll a dice)

If they shoot, all goalkeepers have a 1 in 12 chance of being on target.

If a goalkeeper scores, it is worth **3 goals**.

- **Midfielders can**:
    - Tackle (roll a dice)
    - Pass to strikers
    - Shoot (roll a dice)

If they shoot, all midfielders have a 1 in 6 chance of being on target.

If a midfielder scores, it is worth **2 goals**.

- **Strikers can**:
    - Shoot (roll a dice)

When a striker shoots, their chance of being on target depends on their probability rating.

If strikers score, it is worth **1 goal**.

Player lists for auction — Four-a-side football

■ This data has been provided for teachers who do not have access to an interactive whiteboard for the session. The information below covers 32 footballers, for a maximum of 8 teams. **Maximum budget per team = £6 million.**

Position	Name	Suggested value	Key skill	Long shots: chance of being on target
Goalkeepers	Carina the Cat	£2.3 million	2 in 3 chance of saving	1 in 12 (toss a head or a tail on the coin, and roll one nominated number on the dice)
	Luke Longarms	£2.1 million	2 in 3 chance of saving	
	Samantha Saveit	£1.9 million	50/50 chance of saving	
	Tim Tipitover	£1.7 million	50/50 chance of saving	
	Josie Justawake	£1.3 million	1 in 3 chance of saving	
	Mike Missedit	£1.1 million	1 in 3 chance of saving	
	Diana Droppedit	£0.8 million	1 in 6 chance of saving	
	Bob Butterfingers	£0.5 million	1 in 6 chance of saving	
Left-side midfielders	Clara Cruncher	£2.1 million	2 in 3 chance of tackling	1 in 6 (roll one nominated number on the dice)
	Norman Nofear	£2.0 million	2 in 3 chance of tackling	
	Wanda Wellyit	£1.8 million	50/50 chance of tackling	
	Paul Puntit	£1.6 million	50/50 chance of tackling	
	Sara Slicer	£1.1 million	1 in 3 chance of tackling	
	Dave Diveaway	£1.1 million	1 in 3 chance of tackling	
	Lisa Lazybones	£0.8 million	1 in 6 chance of tackling	
	Tommy Tremble	£0.6 million	1 in 6 chance of tackling	
Right-side midfielders	Suzi Slidetackle	£2.3 million	2 in 3 chance of tackling	1 in 6 (roll one nominated number on the dice)
	Ahmed Alright	£2.2 million	2 in 3 chance of tackling	
	Tina Trappit	£1.9 million	50/50 chance of tackling	
	Kelvin Kickit	£1.7 million	50/50 chance of tackling	
	Hannah Hacker	£1.2 million	1 in 3 chance of tackling	
	Joe Jumpaway	£1.0 million	1 in 3 chance of tackling	
	Roberta Rollover	£0.7 million	1 in 6 chance of tackling	
	Steve Snoozer	£0.6 million	1 in 6 chance of tackling	
Strikers	Sharon Sureshot	£2.5 million	2 in 3 chance on target	Use the striker's key skill probability, and then nominate number(s) on the dice.
	Ronny Rocket	£2.4 million	2 in 3 chance on target	
	Brenda Blastit	£1.8 million	50/50 chance on target	
	Pete Precision	£1.7 million	50/50 chance on target	
	Karen Kneedit	£1.3 million	1 in 3 chance on target	
	Wayne Wildkick	£1.1 million	1 in 3 chance on target	
	Cheri Cleanboots	£0.6 million	1 in 6 chance on target	
	Terry Two-lefts	£0.5 million	1 in 6 chance on target	

REAL-LIFE MATHS Ages 9–11 *Scenario 9*

■ Fill in your players' details then colour the counters in your team's colour and cut them out.

Goalkeeper

GK

Name: _____

Cost: _____

Probability of saving: _____

Probability of shooting on target: 1 in 12

Right midfield

RM

Name: _____

Cost: _____

Probability of tackling: _____

Probability of shooting on target: 1 in 6

Left midfield

LM

Name: _____

Cost: _____

Probability of tackling: _____

Probability of shooting on target: 1 in 6

Striker

S

Name: _____

Cost: _____

Probability of shooting on target: _____

■ Record all your team's results in the chart.

Opponents	Score	Points	Goal difference	Total goal difference	Total points
1					
2					
3					
4					
5					
6					
7					
Totals					

■ Use tally charts like these to track your players' performances through the league.

Position	Name	Saves made	Goals conceded	Shots on target	Shots off target
Goalkeeper					

Position	Name	Tackles won	Tackles lost	Shots on target	Shots off target
Left midfield					

Position	Name	Tackles won	Tackles lost	Shots on target	Shots off target
Right midfield					

Position	Name	Shots on target	Shots off target
Striker			

Dragonmasters

Overview
Using information and formulae, children develop a settlement to resist dragon attacks.

Timescales
- Lesson I (about I hour): Discuss the concepts and rules. Work through the formulae as part of a sample day.
- Lesson 2 (minimum I hour): Children work in small groups to resist a single dragon attack.
- Further lessons (minimum I hour): Children can trade with each other if desired, and then resist the attacks of all four dragons and try to become Dragonmasters.
- Extension: Challenge more confident children to set up spreadsheets to calculate their resource allocations.

Maths covered
- Using formulae.
- Using four operations up to and over 1000.
- Logical presentation of work and strategic thinking.

Prior learning
Children should understand simple algebraic formula and be comfortable with all four operations.

Cross-curricular links
- Literacy: speaking and listening.
- PSHE: cooperation.

CD-ROM resources list
- Scenario video and slideshow.
- Photocopiables: *Scenario guidelines, Information sheet, Daily resource tracking sheet.*

Resource list
Pencils, paper, calculators (optional).

Setting the scene
Watch the introductory video on the CD-ROM and explain to the class that they will take the role of the leaders of a small settlement in the land of Dragonia, where dragons are returning. In Lesson I, guide children through the rules, the dragons, and the formulae involved. Work through the example on the photocopiable *Info sheet – dragons and formulae.* Model how to record the ongoing numbers each day. Discuss how children will need to consider carefully requirements over the whole period of six days. In particular, they must ensure: they have enough food for the seventh day; that shelters are built within six days; and that none of the settlers are ever idle or do wasted work.

Running the scenario
When you are confident that children understand the task, arrange them in groups and give each group a copy of the *Scenario guidelines* and *Daily resource tracking* sheet. Start the scenario running on the interactive whiteboard. This counts down the days, culminating in the dragon attack on 'Day 7'. Allow around 10 minutes on 'Day I' for groups to discuss their strategy, then 5 minutes for each subsequent day. Setting time limits helps avoid procrastination and creates more tension and focus, though you may give more time if necessary. On the 'day of attack' check all calculations. To get the most benefit from this activity, carry amounts from 'Day 7' over to the next week. Remember to add (or maybe remove) new settlers as per the guidelines, and prepare for harder dragon attacks. If the activity is going well, you might also encourage different groups to trade resources after each 'week'. Can children survive all four attacks and become Dragonmasters?

Differentiation
Less confident learners could use a calculator to assist them.
More confident learners should perform all calculations mentally.

Review
Ask children to share their work with each other. Are their calculations accurate? What strategies did they find were useful? What was difficult? What would they do differently next time?

Further ideas
Introduce board games or computer games that are based on building settlements.

Scenario guidelines — Dragonmasters

Dragonia

Dragonia, a beautiful land with a terrible problem. Once upon a time, it was a land of dragons, but slowly people drove them away, until nothing was left but rumours. These days people can scarcely believe it was true – dragons indeed!

But news has come that the dragons really are returning, and they want this land for themselves. They are well organised, coming in one-weekly intervals, the weakest dragon to the strongest. You cannot fight them. You can only protect yourselves from their attacks, leaving them too weak to challenge you for a year or more, such is their slow rate of recovery.

A village elder has the sacred scroll, containing the secret formula that will help you to prepare, and to fend off the dragons.

People and jobs

- To begin, there are 100 settlers in your settlement, and no resources at all.
- Every person must have one meal a day. A meal is one fish and 1kg of grain.
- For every meal short of 100 on any day, a settler cannot work the next day.
- You can store as much fish and grain as you want to, for use on future days.
- You can carry over spare resources to the next week.

Dragon attacks

- On the day of attack (Day 7), no one can work, but everyone must eat as usual.
- On the day of attack, all calculations are checked. For every error, five settlers must leave your settlement for ever. They will not be able to help you for the next attack.
- After a dragon attack, news of your secure settlement spreads. For every five settlers still alive in your settlement, one new settler will come and join you.
- You will need more than 100 settlers to fend off the bigger dragons.

The shelters

- Different strength shelters are needed for different dragons.
- The shelters you build can hold five settlers at the most.
- If you have too few shelters on the day of attack, you lose settlers. For every missing shelter, you lose five settlers.
- You must build fresh shelters for the next dragon attack. Previous shelters are scorched and weak.

Calculations and tips

- You cannot build part-shelters, chop down half-trees, and so on. Always round numbers down.
- You cannot go back and change a previous day's work.
- You must use the given formula, and check your work thoroughly.
- Spend time agreeing a strategy; think about what you need to achieve.
- Share out different calculations (for example, number of trees felled), on each day.
- Check one another's calculations.

1. Fledgling

50 trees are needed to build a strong enough shelter for every five settlers.

Fledgling is the youngest of the dragons. This will be the first time she has left her nest high in the mountains. But beware! Her clumsiness can make her more dangerous.

2. Firebreath

80 trees are needed to build a strong enough shelter for every five settlers.

A reckless male dragon, Firebreath breathes the most powerful flames of all. Shelters that are not strong enough will be burnt to the ground in seconds.

3. Crusher

100 trees are needed to build a strong enough shelter for every five settlers.

Crusher is old, slow and heavy. He attacks using his weight to crush what he lands on. Anything that is not strong enough will collapse under him.

4. Invincible

130 trees are needed to build a strong enough shelter for every five settlers.

Invincible's vast power comes from her armour-plated body that glows with heat. Only the strongest shelters will withstand her blows.

The formulae

Job	Role	Item	Formulae	Letter representations	
catching	to catch fish for food	fish	$f = 10c$	f = fish	c = catchers
harvesting	to grow grain for food	grain (kg)	$g = h^2$	g = grain	h = harvesters
felling	to chop down trees for shelters	trees	$t = 4f$	t = trees	f = fellers
building	to build shelters with the trees	shelters	$s = b \div 8$	s = shelters	b = builders

Sample calculations

Week 1, day 1: 100 settlers available   Dragon = Fledgling   50 trees needed per shelter.

Look carefully and make sure you understand the example. Can you plan and calculate the next day?

Day 1	c = 15	h = 12	f = 49	b = 24
Gains	f = 150	g = 144	t = 196	s = 3
Losses	−100	−100	−150	0
Total	50	44	46	3
Day 2	c =	h =	f =	b =
Gains	f =	g =	t =	s =
Losses				
Total				

Daily resource tracking sheet — Dragonmasters

Settlement name: _____

Week: _____ Dragon: _____

Trees needed per shelter: _____

Number of settlers: _____

Job	Item	Formula
c = catchers	f = fish	f = 10c
h = harvesters	g = grain (kg)	$g = h^2$
f = fellers	t = trees	t = 4f
b = builders	s = shelters	s = b ÷ 8

Day 1	c =	h =	f =	b =
Gains	f =	g =	t =	s =
Losses				
Total				
Day 2	c =	h =	f =	b =
Gains	f =	g =	t =	s =
Losses				
Total				
Day 3	c =	h =	f =	b =
Gains	f =	g =	t =	s =
Losses				
Total				
Day 4	c =	h =	f =	b =
Gains	f =	g =	t =	s =
Losses				
Total				
Day 5	c =	h =	f =	b =
Gains	f =	g =	t =	s =
Losses				
Total				
Day 6	c =	h =	f =	b =
Gains	f =	g =	t =	s =
Losses				
Total				
Day 7	**Dragon attack** – no gains on Day 7			
Day 7 losses				
Resources to carry forward to next week	f =	g =	t =	s =

Tips and ideas

While it might be too time-consuming for teachers to develop resources like those in this book, there are many opportunities to develop meaningful maths into engaging lessons. First and foremost, remember that 'word problems' are fine, but they are not the same as scenario-based activities where the maths is an integral part rather than an end in itself. As such, the following checklist and ideas have been provided as a starting point for developing your own activities:

Consider the context – make sure the activities use maths in a meaningful way.

Consider cross-curricular links – think about how maths is involved in each area of the curriculum.

Money Money Money – given that most maths we do in adult life centres around money, there should be no problem developing new ideas around cash.

Differentiation – this is the trickiest part of developing your own resources. Do you want to really challenge children, or to consolidate their existing skills? (A mixture of both is recommended over time.)

Presenting work – how children present their work is very important for successful real-life maths work. Consider whether you want children to follow tight guidelines or allow them more freedom. The latter is particularly liberating for those used to laying out work in prescriptive ways.

Discussing work – we allow children to look at and discuss each other's literacy and topic work, so why not their maths? Talking about how they have presented their work, as well as the actual maths, can consolidate understanding.

Starting points

Your school:
- Challenge children to plan the itinery, budgets and general logistics for school trips.
- Does the school have a playground? What is the area of the playground? If it needed resurfacing how much would it cost? What about markings, equipment and seating?
- Do the children have a school uniform? How much does it cost compared to their favourite clothes? What are the financial benefits of having one, if any?
- Introduce new playground games and set up leagues for them. Have older children monitor results, league places and so on.
- Monitor energy usage in the class or the school. How much do the annual bills cost? Could the school save money?

Children's lives:
- Don't just ask children to write about their holidays. Delve into the distances travelled, time taken, and so on. Or, plan dream holidays, complete with budgets, timetables and logistics.
- Use brochures to design a dream bedroom. What would it cost?
- Track the children's diet. How many calories are consumed? How far did the food travel to reach their plate? How environmentally friendly are their meals?

Charity and enterprise:
- Support children in running stalls and events to raise funds for charities.
- Run your own Scholastic Book Fair to raise funds: **www.bookfairs.scholastic.co.uk/business_school**